A
Study Guide

JEWISH
FOUNDATIONS
Sacrifice, Worship, and the Messiah

A DVD-based study series
Study Guide

JEWISH FOUNDATIONS

Sacrifice, Worship, and the Messiah

With Mart De Haan

Eight Lessons for Group Exploration

DISCOVERY HOUSE

PUBLISHERS®

Feeding the Soul with the Word of God

The DayLight Bible Studies are based on programs produced by
Day of Discovery, **a Bible-teaching TV series of RBC Ministries.**

© 2011 by Discovery House Publishers

Discovery House Publishers is affiliated with RBC Ministries,
Grand Rapids, Michigan.

Requests for permission to quote from this book should be directed to:
Permissions Department
Discovery House Publishers
P.O. Box 3566
Grand Rapids, MI 49501
or email us at permissionsdept@dhp.org

Study questions by Andrew Sloan
Interior design by Sherri L. Hoffman
Cover design by Jeremy Culp
Cover photo by iStockphoto

ISBN: 978-1-57293-536-5

Printed in the United States of America

First printing in 2011

CONTENTS

Introduction: Not a Pretty Picture   7

SESSION 1
The Problem with Sacrifices   9

SESSION 2
The Great Exchange   17

SESSION 3
Connecting with the Temple   25

SESSION 4
A Walk Through the Temple   33

SESSION 5
The Great Divide   41

SESSION 6
Understanding "Messiah"   49

SESSION 7
Contrasting Images of Messiah   57

SESSION 8
Who Is This Messiah?   65

INTRODUCTION

Not a Pretty Picture

There's something rather messy about Christianity. When you read the book that reveals the background of the faith—the Old Testament we call it—you are forced to slog through all kinds of rituals and practices that seem to lack a twenty-first-century sophistication.

Over and over and over, we read about cute, cuddly animals that are slain and butchered and offered up as sacrifices. Lambs. Sheep. Bulls. Goats.

All manner of farm animals that we love to pet and feed and watch frolic in fields of clover are slain for religious purposes.

It's all kind of messy and gross.

You might think, *I can't wait to get to the New Testament so all this stuff will stop.* But then you get to the end of the gospels of Matthew, Mark, and Luke—and things get even worse.

Instead of animals giving up their lives in bloody sacrifices, the unthinkable happens: A man is horribly and grotesquely killed. And we discover that His death is something that could seem to be right out of the tales of a pagan religion. This man is a human sacrifice.

No, it's not a pretty picture. An Old Testament that requires animal sacrifice if the people want to be in a relationship with God—followed by a human sacrifice that is necessary in order for sins of the people to be forgiven.

What are we to make of all this? How does it all tie together to create what eventually becomes a marvelous picture of God's perfect plan? How do the activities and practices of a group of people known as Jews meld together into the beliefs of a new sect of believers who would come to be called Christians? What are the connections that knit those two seemingly separate faiths together to create the gospel of Jesus Christ?

Three men from widely disparate backgrounds met together in the land of the Bible to answer some of those questions. One man, a Gentile, grew up in a family of strong, Bible-believing Christians. Another man, a Jew, was trained in the United States and lives in Beersheba, Israel, where he serves as a tour guide. The third, also Jewish, grew up in Israel and speaks English as a second language to his native Hebrew. All three embrace New Testament Christianity but value the heritage of Old Testament truth.

Together, Mart De Haan, Avner Boskey, and Meno Kalisher, visit several locations in Israel to examine the reality that historic Jewish history and faith—with its background of sacrifices, its history of tabernacle/temple worship, and its promise of a coming Messiah—flows into the New Covenant teaching of a man named Jesus, who become a human sacrifice for all of mankind.

As they explore the Old Testament sacrificial system, they help us see that God's intricate plan leads directly to the cross. And as they explore the implements and furniture in the tabernacle of the wandering children of Israel and the temple of the Jews living in the Land of Promise, they assist us in understanding how clearly the sometimes messy story of sacrifices points to a Savior through the symbols, the rituals, and the promises that found fulfillment in the New Testament.

Christianity isn't always pretty. But it is beautiful. It provides hope, healing, and a future—all based on Jewish foundations carefully planned and arranged by God's sovereign hand.

—Dave Branon
Editor

The Problem with Sacrifices

DAYLIGHT PREVIEW

Systems of Sacrifices

Christians, Jews, and pagans all have utilized sacrifices down through the ages as they conducted their worship. As troubling as that connection might seem, it is possible to see the distinction that makes all the difference. Pagan worshipers saw their sacrifices—which included the offering of children on the altar—as appeasement to their gods. Jewish communities were instructed to sacrifice animals during their worship as a covering for sin. And the Christian faith centers on the sacrifice of a human—the Man Jesus, who voluntarily gave his life for us. Mart De Haan, Avner Boskey, and Meno Kalisher examine what is behind the systems and why one of them has saving power today.

COME TOGETHER

Icebreaker Questions

1. Have you ever worn a cross bracelet or necklace? Do you wear one now? Why or why not?

2. This session takes place at the Valley of Hinnom, or Gehenna, where the residents of Jerusalem used to burn their garbage. Have you ever visited a place like that in a country where the citizens burn their garbage dumps?

3. In this series we are considering the Jewish roots of our Christian faith. How would you describe your family's religious or spiritual roots?

 FINDING DAYLIGHT

Experience the Video

Feel free to jot down Video Notes as you watch the presentation by Mart De Haan, Avner Boskey, and Meno Kalisher. Use the space below for those notes.

——————————————VIDEO NOTES——————————————

The cross

Avner and Meno

Gehenna

Topheth

Pagan vs. Christian

Bridge between man and God

Isaiah 53: Guilt offering

Korban = sacrifice

 WALKING IN THE DAYLIGHT

Discussion Time

——————— DISCOVER GOD'S WORD ———————

Discussion/Application Questions

1. As we think about studying the Jewish foundation of Christianity, do you tend to think of Christianity as an outgrowth of the Jewish faith or as a new and separate religion?

2. Mart De Haan begins this session by saying, "In our day many regard even animal sacrifice as being unthinkable, let alone human sacrifice, which has become a real problem for those who have thought about the fact that ritual sacrifice was central to the Jewish temple—and not only to the Jewish temple but also to the Christian gospel that emphasizes that Jesus died as a human sacrifice for our sins. Today, all over Jerusalem and around the world, Christian houses of worship

are identified by that cross. It's a cross cherished by followers of Jesus but repulsive to those who see human sacrifice as an act of pagan ignorance and savagery."

a. Have you ever thought of Jesus' death on the cross in terms of a human sacrifice?

b. How can we, as followers of Christ, defend our love of the cross?

3. **This session begins in a beautiful valley, an area that has witnessed the worst kinds of tragedies. Read what the prophet Jeremiah had to say about that valley in Jeremiah 7:30–31.**

The word *topheth*, which is of Aramaic origin, means "fireplace." Outside of Israel it was also used as a common noun for a place of child sacrifice.

How had the people of Judah broken their covenant with the Lord?

4. **Read Jeremiah's pronouncement of judgment in regard to this valley in Jeremiah 7:32–34.**

Jeremiah prophesied the future destruction of Judah at the hands of the Babylonians. This valley of child sacrifice would become a cemetery when the people of Judah were slaughtered by the invading Babylonian army. How would that history—along with the fact that this was a garbage dump where there was always the smell of burning garbage—contribute to the emotional effect when Jesus would later refer to hell as Gehenna, the "Valley of Hinnom"?

5. **Even though child sacrifice was prohibited in the law of Moses (Leviticus 18:21; Deuteronomy 18:10), some Israelites practiced this horrible rite. Notice that two of Judah's kings, Ahaz (read 2 Kings 16:2–3) and Manasseh (read 2 Kings 21:1–6), sacrificed their children.**

   a. How do you suppose these two men, descendants of David, could have done such a thing?

   b. What's the difference between this kind of sacrifice and the animal sacrifices prescribed in the Old Testament, which in turn lead up to the sacrifice of Christ?

6. **The prophet Isaiah, who lived seven hundred years before Christ, foretold the suffering of God's Messiah. Read Isaiah 53:10–11.**

   A "guilt offering," or "offering for sin," was employed in situations such as theft or cheating—in which restitution was possible. In addition to returning the stolen property, the offender sacrificed a ram.

   In what way was Jesus our "guilt offering"?

7. What does Meno mean when he says that the principle of sacrifice is always "life for life"? How does that help explain Christ's death on the cross?

—————————— BRINGING IT HOME ——————————

1. What do you hope to gain from this study and from spending time with this group?

2. Have you known anyone for whom the idea of blood sacrifice has been a barrier or hang-up in regard to Christianity? Has that ever been an issue for you?

3. Avner Boskey and Meno Kalisher point out that the pagan concept of sacrifice (for example, the worship of Baal in the Old Testament) is to pay a god so that he will give you what you need and want. Avner observes that some Christians have that attitude toward God as well.

    a. What do you think Avner means?

    b. Can you identify with relating to God in that way?

DAYLIGHT ON PRAYER

Spending Time with God

1. How can the group support your relationship with God in prayer?

2. Do you have any other prayer requests to share with the group?

DAYLIGHT AHEAD

After Meno Kalisher explains clearly what happens in a Jewish sacrifice—using Avner as his "sheep"—the scene shifts to an actual Jewish ceremony in which a sheep is offered up as a sacrifice. The discussion moves, then, to an examination of why this happens—why sacrifices are so vital to the Christian faith. And it all comes back to one thing: The need for sacrifice is closely related to our sinfulness and a need for forgiveness.

The Great Exchange

DAYLIGHT PREVIEW

Embracing Sacrifice?

This whole messy idea of making sacrifices can, as Mart De Haan says, "sound horrendous" to some people. How can those people—ones who might be repulsed by the idea—be made to understand its significance? With the passion of people who have grown up Jewish and who understand the Jewish sacrificial system of the Old Testament, Meno Kalisher and Avner Boskey explain and demonstrate the value of the system. They explain why this great exchange pictures Jesus' sacrifice for mankind.

COME TOGETHER

Icebreaker Questions

1. What's the biggest bonfire you can remember?

2. In this session Meno Kalisher compels Avner Boskey to role-play the part of a sacrificial lamb. Have you ever played the part of an animal in a Christmas pageant or some other play?

3. The focus of this session (like the last session) is on sacrifice. Name one sacrifice you have made or a sacrifice someone else has made for you.

FINDING DAYLIGHT

Experience the Video

Feel free to jot down Video Notes as you watch the presentation by Mart De Haan, Avner Boskey, and Meno Kalisher. Use the space below for those notes.

───────────────── VIDEO NOTES ─────────────────

The temple and Jewish life

Atonement: A sacrificial lamb

The exchange

Why is sacrifice necessary?

Problem of sin: actions and thoughts

Repeated sacrifices vs. Jesus' sacrifice

The geography outside Jerusalem

Making the turn

Pentecost and Peter's sermon

Mart's summary

WALKING IN THE DAYLIGHT

Discussion Time

————— DISCOVER GOD'S WORD —————
Discussion/Application Questions

1. **As this session begins, Mart, Meno, and Avner imagine what it would have been like to come to the temple to present an animal sacrifice.**

   a. How do you think you would have felt if you had been a Jewish pilgrim in Jesus' day and as you approached Jerusalem you saw the temple, looming perhaps seventeen stories high, with smoke wafting above it due to the constant ritual sacrifices?

b. How do you think you would have felt when you arrived at the temple to present a sacrifice to God—placing your hands on the lamb's head and then killing it by slitting its throat?

c. Then imagine, as Meno suggests, that your ten-year-old child asks you, "What have you done?" What answer would you give?

2. **Read what the law of Moses, in Leviticus 17:10–12, says about a couple of significant principles.**

   The Lord notes that "the life of a creature is in the blood" (v. 11). Both animal and human life is a special gift from God, and people were not to try to enhance the life force within them by eating the "life" contained in blood, as many pagan people believed they could do. Since the blood shed in sacrifices was sacred, representing as it did the life of the sacrificial victim, that blood must be treated with respect. And as a result, eating blood was strictly prohibited.

   a. What do you think God meant when He said, "It is the blood that makes atonement for one's life" (v. 11)?

   b. How does Hebrews 9:22—"Without the shedding of blood there is no forgiveness"—reinforce this principle?

3. The Lord decreed that Israel's high priest should enter the Holy of Holies, or Most Holy Place, once a year, in September or October, to atone for the people's sins. Read about this Day of Atonement (Yom Kippur) in Leviticus 16:2, 11–19.

    Avner points out that word *kippur* means "covering." What does Avner mean that the blood of bulls and goats once a year couldn't fully remove sins but only "cover" them?

4. Read how Hebrews 7:23–28 in the New Testament speaks to this.

    How was Christ's sacrifice able to be "once for all"?

5. In response to Mart's question about how Jewish people first made the turn from offering animal sacrifices to accepting Jesus as the Lamb of God, Meno referred to the day of Pentecost, fifty days after Jesus' resurrection, when the Holy Spirit filled the first believers and Peter had the opportunity to tell the crowd about salvation through the Messiah. Read Acts 2:22–24.

    a. According to Peter, what was the crowd already aware of in regard to Jesus?

    b. What responsibility did Peter seem to place upon the crowd? (Note: Peter's reference to "wicked men" could be translated "those not having the law"—that is, Gentiles.)

6. Read Acts 2:32–41 to see how this scene concludes.

    In verse 35, Peter was quoting Psalm 110. According to Peter, David was speaking of his descendant with tremendous respect: "The Lord [God] said to my Lord [the Messiah] . . ." In addition to being resurrected (vv. 31–32), the Messiah would be exalted to God's right hand and pour out the Holy Spirit, an event that had just occurred (v. 33).

    What effect did Peter's words have on the crowd? How did they respond?

————————————— BRINGING IT HOME —————————————

1. Have you ever felt "cut to the heart" (Acts 2:37) when comparing who you are to who Jesus is?

2. How did you make the turn from going your own selfish and sinful way to following Jesus as the Lamb of God?

3. How do you feel about the spiritual path you're on now?

DAYLIGHT ON PRAYER

Spending Time with God

1. How can the group support you in prayer at this juncture in your spiritual journey?

2. What other prayer requests would you like to share with the group?

3. As you close, give Jesus thanks and praise for being our "once for all" sacrifice.

DAYLIGHT AHEAD

What do you know about the temple that once stood in Jerusalem? And what connection could there possibly be between that ancient building and the church today? Mart De Haan, Avner Boskey, and Meno Kalisher visit the oldest Christian church in the old city of Jerusalem to talk about that question. They examine the idea that the Jewish foundations of spirituality rooted in the temple do indeed carry over to the Christian church.

SESSION 3

Connecting with the Temple

DAYLIGHT PREVIEW

From the Tabernacle to the Temple to Today

Thousands of years ago, God gave Moses the exact plans for building the tabernacle, the moveable worship center of the Jewish people. Later, those plans were used to construct a more permanent location—the temple in Jerusalem. But did it stop there? Were the symbols that furnished the tabernacle/temple just for people 2,000 years ago and earlier? Or can we see spiritual teaching and benefit from those symbols in the Christian church today? That's the question Mart De Haan is asking, and Meno Kalisher and Avner Boskey want to help him answer it.

COME TOGETHER

Icebreaker Questions

1. This session begins at the golden menorah in Jerusalem, which Mart compares with an American national symbol, the Liberty Bell in Philadelphia. What visit to a national symbol stands out in your memory?

2. What memories do you have of losing your electricity and using candles for light?

3. During this session, Mart, Avner, and Meno visit Christ Church in Jeru-
    salem, an Anglican church that was designed to make Jewish people
    feel comfortable. Though we know the "church" is the people, not the
    building, what is one of the most warm and inviting church buildings
    you have worshiped in?

 FINDING DAYLIGHT

Experience the Video

Feel free to jot down Video Notes as you watch the presentation by Mart
De Haan, Avner Boskey, and Meno Kalisher. Use the space below for those
notes.

──────────────── VIDEO NOTES ────────────────

The temple

The menorah

Inside the temple

Symbolism of temple

Christ's Church, Jerusalem

Meno's warning

Tabernacle/temple

WALKING IN THE DAYLIGHT

Discussion Time

—————————— DISCOVER GOD'S WORD ——————————

Discussion/Application Questions

1. **Mart, Avner, and Meno begin this session at the golden menorah replica in Jerusalem's Jewish quarter, not far from where the temple once stood. Read Exodus 25:31–40 to see how the Lord told Moses to make the lampstand for the Holy Place inside the tabernacle (and subsequently inside the temple).**

   Although the Scriptures don't clearly specify the meaning of the lampstand's function or design, what might the following suggest:

   a. Its composition of pure gold?

b. Its design in the pattern of an almond tree, the first tree in the Promised Land to blossom each spring?

c. Its makeup of seven lamps (v. 37)?

d. Its function of burning all night, tended for by the priests who used olive oil provided by the people (Exodus 27:20–21)?

2. **Read an earlier passage from Exodus 25—verses 1–9. The setting was the foot of Mount Sinai after God delivered the Israelites from bondage in Egypt.**

a. Why do you think God wanted the Israelites to make a tabernacle?

b. Was that the only way He could "dwell" among His people?

3. **Read how Hebrews 8:3–5 in the New Testament follows up on this. Hebrews 8:5 quotes Exodus 25:40, which is nearly identical to Exodus 25:9.**

a. What do you think the writer of Hebrews means by saying that the tabernacle is "a copy and shadow of what is in heaven"? What does Avner mean, in this regard, when he says that there was a kind of "on earth as it is in heaven" construction of the tabernacle and then later the temple?

b. How does the tabernacle of the old covenant compare with the "high priest" (Christ) of the new covenant?

4. **Meno and Mart assert that the concepts and symbolism of the temple have come into the church in ways that we don't often consider. Can you think of examples of how this is true?**

5. **Mart asks the question, "Can we get the whole pattern and the symbolism of the temple into the church in a way that's meaningful to us? Or are we contriving things?" How would you answer that question?**

6. **Meno answers Mart's question in the affirmative, but adds a caution: God wants an intimate relationship with people, not the furniture. "The furniture is beautiful, but the church is not chairs, stones, and furniture. The church is us—born-again believers. We are living stones. God dwells in us. We are the temple of God."**

   In light of this, read 1 Peter 2:9–10.

   a. How does this passage support Meno's statement that God wants an intimate relationship with people, not the furniture?

b. How does this passage speak to Mart's question about whether we can get the whole pattern and the symbolism of the temple into the church?

7. **Along these lines, read 1 Corinthians 3:16.**

How does this verse speak to Mart's question about whether we can get the whole pattern and the symbolism of the temple into the church?

──────────────── BRINGING IT HOME ────────────────

1. **Do religious symbols tend to draw your attention toward God or away from God?**

2. **Light is a common metaphor in the Scriptures. The book of Revelation (1:9–20) likens seven churches to seven golden lampstands. Jesus said, "I am the light of the world" (John 8:12). And He also told those who follow Him, "You are the light of world" (Matthew 5:14). Clearly churches and individual believers are supposed to reflect the light of God's presence in a dark world.**

Do you remember the children's song, "This little light of mine, I'm gonna let it shine"? On a scale of 1 to 10, how brightly is your light shining?

DAYLIGHT ON PRAYER

Spending Time with God

1. How can the group pray for your "light" to shine brighter?

2. Do you have a personal prayer request to share? What other people and needs are you concerned about?

3. Spend time together as a group praying for each other and your concerns. Close by thanking God for fashioning us as living stones and as the temple of God in whom God dwells.

DAYLIGHT AHEAD

Christ Church in Jerusalem, built by British Christians in the nineteenth century, remains the focus of Mart, Avner, and Meno as they continue to examine the reality that the Christian faith rests squarely on a Jewish foundation. They discuss the furniture of the temple and how those items represent vital elements of Christianity: washing at the basin, sacrifices at the altar, incense representing prayers, and other items. Each of these show that connection between Judaism and Christianity.

A Walk Through the Temple

DAYLIGHT PREVIEW

Symbols Revealed

While the Christian church you attend may not put much emphasis on icons and symbols, you might be surprised to discover that a complete understanding of the background of the faith must include symbolic objects. It was God himself who directed Moses to include symbols in the tabernacle and later the temple—objects that can still point us to truths we cherish as followers of Jesus. Avner Boskey and Meno Kalisher point out those symbols to Mart De Haan, and us, as a reminder of the complete picture of God's plan of salvation.

——————— COME TOGETHER ———————

Icebreaker Questions

1. During this session Meno humorously points out how noteworthy it is that two Jews (Meno and Avner) agree on an issue! Who did you have trouble agreeing with when you were growing up?

2. In the video we learn about the table of showbread. What's the best bread you can ever remember eating?

3. At the end of this session Mart reflects that their conversation at Christ Church was in some ways like a family reunion, where shared experiences were retold and fondly remembered. What do you think of when you recall your own past family reunions?

 ## FINDING DAYLIGHT

Experience the Video

Feel free to jot down Video Notes as you watch the presentation by Mart De Haan, Avner Boskey, and Meno Kalisher. Use the space below for those notes.

——————————VIDEO NOTES——————————

Church-temple links

Lord's Supper

Foot washing

Pattern of the tabernacle/temple

Bronze basin

Altar of sacrifice

Holy Place

Table of showbread, incense altar, lampstand

Holy of Holies

Through the veil

The blood on the ark

The Law prepared us for Christ

Jesus: The son of David

A pattern, a sacrifice, a light—preparing us for Jesus

Mart's summary: A family reunion

 WALKING IN THE DAYLIGHT

Discussion Time

─────────── **DISCOVER GOD'S WORD** ───────────

Discussion/Application Questions

1. **This session begins with Meno making a connection between the temple and the church in terms of the Lord's Supper. Read Matthew 26:26–28.**

    a. What connection do you see here between the temple and the church, between Judaism and Christianity?

    b. What do you think about Meno's statement that "when we take the Lord's Supper it's like presenting a sacrifice"?

2. Mart asks Avner to "go up a couple of thousand feet" and look at the overall pattern of the tabernacle and the temple. Avner notes that as you would look down on the tabernacle or temple, the first thing you would see would be a huge bronze basin, also known as a laver or sea. Read about that basin in Exodus 30:17–21.

   a. What connection do you see here between the temple and the church, between Judaism and Christianity?

   b. What do you think about Avner connecting the basin with Christian baptism?

3. The next thing you would see would be the bronze altar where the sacrifices were offered up to God. Read about that altar in Exodus 27:1–8.

   What connection do you see here between the temple and the church, between Judaism and Christianity?

4. Now we come to the Holy Place, which only the priests could enter, where we find the lampstand (which we considered in the last session), the table of showbread (also known as "the bread of the Presence"), and the incense altar. Read about the lampstand and the table of showbread in Leviticus 24:1–9.

   The twelve loaves of bread were a gift from the twelve tribes of Israel, apparently communicating both the people's recognition that

God provided for their needs and an offering back to Him from the fruit of their labor.

What connection do you see here between the temple and the church, between Judaism and Christianity?

5. **Now read about the incense altar in Exodus 30:1–10.**

    Other Scriptures (Psalm 141:2; Revelation 5:8; 8:3–4) tell us that the fragrant smoke of incense symbolizes the prayers of God's people. Why do you think that would be the case?

6. **Finally, we come to the Holy of Holies, or Most Holy Place, which only the high priest could enter—and that just once a year, on the Day of Atonement. At that time the high priest would pass through the curtain, or veil, and sprinkle sacrificial blood on the atonement cover, or "mercy seat," between the wings of the cherubim over the ark of the covenant. Read what Hebrews 10:19–22 has to say about entering that holy chamber.**

    What makes it possible for us to go through the curtain, so to speak, and enter God's holy presence?

BRINGING IT HOME

1. **Meno observes that when the people of Israel brought sacrifices to God but not their hearts as well, the Lord said, in essence, "Take it back. I don't want it. Don't defile my temple. I don't need your meat. Go, take care of the poor. Go, take care of the widow. Go, take care of the foreign worker. Take care of them. Love them. Lift them up."**

    a. How can we likewise be guilty of doing the right religious activities without having our hearts in the right place?

    b. Are you involved somehow in taking care of the poor, widows, orphans, and/or foreigners? What ideas does the group have about how to get involved?

2. **Avner connects the bronze altar with Romans 12:1, where Paul tells believers "to offer your bodies as living sacrifices, holy and pleasing to God."**

    a. What do you think Paul means?

    b. How do you go about doing that on a daily basis?

DAYLIGHT ON PRAYER

Spending Time with God

1. How can the group pray for you to more faithfully and effectively obey Romans 12:1 by "offering your body to God as a living sacrifice"?

2. What other prayer requests would you like to share with your group?

3. As you pray, lift up to the Lord people and situations of great need—e.g., the poor, widows, orphans, and foreigners, in general, and world crises in particular.

DAYLIGHT AHEAD

Jewish by birth and Christian by faith, Meno Kalisher and Avner Boskey view things differently from how Mart De Haan, Gentile by birth and Christian by faith, views things. That's the friendly banter that begins the next session as these men discuss the Messiah himself. Is Christianity an extension of Judaism, a natural result—or is it a new thing altogether? It's a fascinating question, and these three will set out to answer that question in Session 5.

The Great Divide

DAYLIGHT PREVIEW

Jewish Christianity?

Avner Boskey begins Session 5 with a declaration that might sound a little strange: "When Christianity began, everyone thought it was Jewish. Two thousand years ago." Then Meno Kalisher chips in with "basic Christianity is pure Judaism." What are these men talking about? Aren't these two faiths totally at odds? Or are they onto something we've lost in the translation and in the pages of history? Mart De Haan, Avner, and Meno explore how the shadows of the Old Testament have been enlightened and fulfilled in the New Testament.

COME TOGETHER
Icebreaker Questions

1. In the beginning of this session, Mart finds a piece of pottery that Avner thinks might be from the time of Jesus. What's the oldest or most fascinating "artifact" you can remember finding?

2. In this session Mart notes that as the Hebrew word "Messiah" was translated into other languages, an important link to Jewish roots was lost in translation. Have you ever studied a foreign language? If so, how much got "lost in translation"?

3. In this session Mart, Avner, and Meno discuss the question of whether the first followers of Christ intended to begin a new religion. Have you or a member of your family ever changed religions? How much stress did that cause in your family?

 FINDING DAYLIGHT

Experience the Video

Feel free to jot down Video Notes as you watch the presentation by Mart De Haan, Avner Boskey, and Meno Kalisher. Use the space below for those notes.

―――――――――――――VIDEO NOTES―――――――――――――

Christianity as a Jewish concept

"It doesn't feel Jewish"

A fulfillment

The wise men

Herod's response

Micah 5:2

Christ: Anointed one and Messiah

Lost in translation

The followers in Antioch

WALKING IN THE DAYLIGHT

Discussion Time

——————————— DISCOVER GOD'S WORD ———————————

Discussion/Application Questions

1. What do you think Mart meant when he said to Meno and Avner, "I talk about Christ and I talk about Christianity—and it doesn't feel Jewish, right?"

2. Do you agree with Meno that "basic Christianity is pure Judaism"? Why or why not?

3. What are the ramifications of Meno's observation that Jesus' disciples, the first generation of Jews who believed in Jesus, didn't intend to start a new religion?

4. Mart notes that the idea that the first followers of Christ had no intention of starting a new faith seems to be in line with the gospel of Matthew. Read, for example, Matthew 1:18–2:6.

   Matthew quoted from Isaiah 7:14 in 1:23 and from Micah 5:2 in 2:6. And his comment in 1:22 that "All this took place to fulfill what the Lord had said through the prophet" was the first of twelve instances in which Matthew stated that the Jewish Scriptures were fulfilled in the story of Jesus.

   How do these circumstances reinforce the point that the first followers of Christ had no intention of beginning a new religion?

5. Avner recounts that as the gospel spread outside of Israel the Hebrew word *Messiah*, or *Mashiach*, with its background in the Old Testament and Judaism, was translated as *Kristos*, or "Christ."

   How damaging do you think this loss in translation has been?

6. **Read Acts 11:19–26, which contains the story of the first mostly Gentile church, as well as the introduction of Paul (Saul) to apostolic ministry among Gentiles.**

   a. The first Christians were forced out of Jerusalem by persecution (see Acts 8:1). Why do you think they confined their proclamation of the gospel to Jews at first?

   b. How does this support the idea that the first followers of Christ had no intention of beginning a new religion?

   c. What convinced Barnabas that the conversion of Gentiles in Antioch was genuine?

7. **Acts 11:26 tells us that the disciples were first called Christians, which means "belonging to Christ" or "Christ people," at Antioch, the third-greatest city of the Roman Empire following Rome and Alexandria. Chances are that this term was coined by the Gentile people of Antioch rather than by the believers themselves—and quite likely in a derisive sense.**

   a. Can you think of ways in which this development of "Christians" as a non-Jewish sect could be a negative thing?

b. Can you think of ways in which this development of "Christians" as a non-Jewish sect could be a positive thing?

BRINGING IT HOME

1. Mart began this session by asking two questions: "How can the followers of two faiths that began as one have so much in common and yet be so far apart? More specifically, how can people who believe in the same Hebrew Scriptures be so far apart on whether Jesus was the promised Jewish Messiah?"

   As Christians, what attitude should we have toward Jews, or people of other faiths for that matter, who don't believe that Jesus was the promised Messiah?

2. In light of Jesus' radical claims about himself, it has been said that there are only four options available for labeling Him: legend, lunatic, liar, or lord. Though many have limited Jesus' identity to that of a great moral teacher, the only option that Jesus himself left open to us, as C. S. Lewis said, is that He is Lord and God.

   How has your understanding of Jesus changed or developed over the years?

DAYLIGHT ON PRAYER

Spending Time with God

1. What do you see as a needed point of growth either in your under-standing of Jesus or your attitude toward people who don't share your view? How can the group pray for you in this regard?

2. Spend some time praying about concerns in your own life as well as burdens you have for others.

DAYLIGHT AHEAD

Historically, what is the importance of Jesus' titles: Messiah and Christ? The older term, *Messiah*, had its origins early in the Old Testament. Later, the term *Christ* was introduced. What does it all mean? Jewish Christians Avner Boskey and Meno Kalisher discuss with Mart De Haan the history of these important terms that are both related to the Savior Jesus.

Understanding "Messiah"

 DAYLIGHT PREVIEW

"Super King"

King of kings, we call Him. And Psalm 89 confirms it. Jesus Christ is the "highest of the kings of the earth" (v. 27). And He is the Messiah. He is the Anointed One—the One who brings salvation to both Jews and Gentiles. Messiah Jesus, as Mart, Avner, and Meno explain, is the source of our salvation, and He will one day return triumphant to Jerusalem. He is indeed the "Super King," as Avner calls Him.

COME TOGETHER

Icebreaker Questions

1. In this session Mart and Avner note how famous and special the Mount of Olives is. What mountain is particularly special to you? Why?

2. This session includes the story of the infant Jesus being dedicated in the temple. Is there a child dedication that stands out in your memory?

3. In this session we get a glimpse of the massive number of graves on the Mount of Olives. How do you feel when you visit a cemetery? Is there a cemetery that has special significance for you? Why?

FINDING DAYLIGHT

Experience the Video

Feel free to jot down Video Notes as you watch the presentation by Mart De Haan, Meno Kalisher, and Avner Boskey. Use the space below for those notes.

─────────────── VIDEO NOTES ───────────────

Meno on the Messiah

The concept of "Messiah"

Anointed ones

The nation is anointed

One personal Messiah

Psalm 89

Anna and Simeon

One idea refined

Moses and Joshua

The Mount of Olives and the Messianic hope

Jesus will return to the Mount of Olives

The prophecy of the coming Messiah

The world's need for the Messiah

The sacrificial lamb

WALKING IN THE DAYLIGHT

Discussion Time

———————DISCOVER GOD'S WORD———————
Discussion/Application Questions

1. With the backdrop of the Kidron Valley and the Mount of Olives, Mart asks the question, "Do you have to be Jewish to appreciate the Messiah?"

    a. What do you think of Meno's answer that a Jew, having been taught the Old Testament, sees many more colors regarding the concept of the Messiah—but on the other hand the danger is thinking that you need to be a Jew in order to be fully saved?

    b. Do you agree with Meno that you don't need to know everything about who Christ is and what He has done as long as you truly know Him?

2. Avner notes that the Hebrew word *messiah* (*mashiach*) has the origin of being God's "anointed one." Kings, prophets, priests—and even the nation of Israel—were all referred to as "anointed ones." But with David we come to the concept of his line forever being the anointed dynasty.

    Read the story of David's anointing in 1 Samuel 16:1–13. (Note: In verse 6, the Hebrew word for the Lord's "anointed" is *mashiach*.)

a. What immediate effect did David's anointing have on him?

b. Although this is the first mention of David in the Bible, what do
    you see in this story—and from what you know about David and
    God's covenant with him—that paves the way for Jesus, the future
    Messiah?

3. **Psalm 89, written many years after David's lifetime, laments the
    demise of David's dynasty and pleads with God for its restoration.
    Read verses 19–29.**

    a. What do you see in this psalm that points to Jesus, the future
        Messiah?

    b. Specifically, how would Jesus fulfill the statement in verse 27 about
        a king who would be "the most exalted of the kings of the earth"?

4. **When Jesus was just a baby, the fact that He was the Messiah was
    confirmed. Read Luke 2:21–38.**

    **According to Leviticus 12, a woman who gave birth to a son was to
    wait forty days before going to the temple to present sacrifices for
    her purification. She was to offer a lamb and either a pigeon or a**

dove. If she couldn't afford a lamb, she could offer two pigeons or two doves.

    a.   What had the Lord revealed to Simeon that he would see before he died?

    b.   How was the awesomeness of this scene intensified by the fact that Jesus was only an infant?

5.   **The prophet Zechariah delivered an amazing prophecy regarding the Mount of Olives and the messianic hope. Read Zechariah 14:2–5.**

    The "holy ones" in verse 5 likely include both believers and angels. Other Scriptures note that they will accompany Christ when He returns (Matthew 25:31; 1 Thessalonians 3:13; Jude 14; Revelation 19:14).

    How does this prophecy of the Messiah's return to the Mount of Olives connect the Jewish messianic hope and the Christian hope?

6.   **It was from the Mount of Olives that Jesus came into Jerusalem on what we call Palm Sunday, declared by adoring crowds as their long-awaited Messiah. Five days later He was crucified. But after His resurrection, Jesus met His disciples one last time on the Mount of Olives. Read about that meeting in Acts 1:1–11. (Note: We know from verse 12 that this took place on the Mount of Olives.)**

    a.   What does the disciples' question in verse 6 reveal about their expectations of the Messiah and His kingdom?

b. What did Jesus' answer reveal about His understanding of the Messiah and His kingdom?

c. How would the promise of the angels in verse 11 fulfill the prophecy of Zechariah 14:4?

————————————— BRINGING IT HOME —————————————

Avner points out that the Old Testament speaks not only of kings, prophets, and priests being anointed but also of the Jewish people. The Lord calls them His "anointed ones" in Psalm 105:15. Meno adds that we as believers today are also anointed for some task.

What job or task do you think God has called you to for the sake of His kingdom?

DAYLIGHT ON PRAYER

Spending Time with God

1. How can the group pray for you in regard to the job or task God has given you?

2. What prayer requests on behalf of yourself or others would you like to share with the group?

3. As you conclude your prayer time, thank God for the promise of Christ's return and the hope that gives us.

 DAYLIGHT AHEAD

Who was this Messiah predicted to come to earth according to the Old Testament Scriptures? The Jewish people were unsure what Messiah would be like when He would appear. According to Avner Boskey, the Jewish people thought there were two coming messiahs. But Isaiah 53 tells us, as Meno Kalisher says, that the Messiah to come was indeed God coming in the flesh. This and other revelations about the coming Messiah are discussed in Session 7 of the study.

Contrasting Images of Messiah

DAYLIGHT PREVIEW

A Tough Call

Imagine reading the prophecies when they were written or in the interven-ing hundreds of years between their writing and Jesus' coming. Would it be easy to figure out exactly what He would be like? For instance, as Mart De Haan points out in this study, Isaiah 53 describes both a conquering king and a suffering servant. Avner Boskey and Meno Kalisher help us see how those contrasting pictures of a coming Messiah were fleshed out in Jewish history—and how they can inform our view today of our Savior, Jesus Christ.

COME TOGETHER

Icebreaker Questions

1. During this session Mart, Avner, and Meno visit the so-called Tomb of Absalom. Have you ever visited a famous tomb?

2. Avner mentions that one Jewish concept of the Messiah is as a conquer-ing hero. Were you a fan of any superheroes when you were a kid?

3. Avner also mentions that many Jews who have longed for the Messiah to come have labored over the words of Scripture, trying to figure out what they mean. What subject in school caused you to "labor" the most?

FINDING DAYLIGHT

Experience the Video

Feel free to jot down Video Notes as you watch the presentation by Mart De Haan, Avner Boskey, and Meno Kalisher. Use the space below for those notes.

————————————VIDEO NOTES————————————

Jesus on the Mount of Olives

How could Jesus fulfill Zechariah?

Jesus' ascension and the promise of a return

Kidron Valley

Maccabean tomb (so-called Tomb of Absalom)

The great hope

Two different messiahs

Isaiah 53

The people were laboring to find Messiah

Isaiah's promise

In the days of Jesus

WALKING IN THE DAYLIGHT

Discussion Time

—————————————— DISCOVER GOD'S WORD ——————————————

Discussion/Application Questions

1. In this session Mart, Meno, and Avner are just a short distance from the Garden of Gethsemane. The New Testament records that Jesus prayed in agony in that olive grove on the lower slopes of the Mount of Olives immediately before He was arrested. Read Mark's account of that story in Mark 14:32–36.

   a. What do we learn about Jesus in terms of His human nature?

   b. What do we learn about Jesus in terms of His knowledge of the future?

   c. What do we learn about Jesus in terms of His relationship with the Father?

2. In the last session, we looked at a prophecy from the book of Zechariah. Read Zechariah 14:4 again.

a. What conclusions about Jesus would you expect a Jewish person in Jesus' day to make when comparing these two scenes from the Mount of Olives?

b. Knowing what we know, how could a crucified Messiah fulfill Zechariah's prediction?

3. **Why do you think that some Jews, as Avner points out, have expected two different Messiahs: one a suffering Messiah and the other a conquering Messiah?**

4. **It's not surprising that the Jewish people recognized within the Old Testament Scriptures some element of suffering in regard to their promised one. Read Isaiah 52:13–53:12. This passage is the last and the longest of the four "servant songs" in the book of Isaiah. Quoted more often by the writers of the New Testament than any other passage in the Jewish Scriptures, it has been called the "gospel in the Old Testament."**

a. Meno states that the language of 52:13 surely describes God. What is the significance of that fact?

b. Mart points out that the prophet Isaiah brings together in this passage the concept of a powerful king and a description of a suffering servant. Where do you see both elements?

c. This passage is much more focused on the description of a suffering servant, but Christ's exaltation is clearly referred to in New Testament passages such as Acts 2:33, Ephesians 1:20–23, and Philippians 2:9–11. Why is it important to emphasize both elements?

5. **Avner mentions that the Jewish people who have longed for the Messiah to come labor to understand God's plan in that regard. Read what 1 Peter 1:10–12 has to say about this.**

a. What do you think Peter meant when he said that the same prophets who predicted the coming of the Messiah searched intently to find the time and circumstances involved?

b. The Holy Spirit can be called the "Spirit of Christ" (verse 11) since Christ sent Him (see John 16:7). What purpose might God have had in leading Peter to write about the irony of the Spirit of Christ working through the prophets to point ahead to the person of Christ?

Just as Isaiah 52:13–53:12 is the classic Old Testament passage about Christ as the suffering servant, Philippians 2:1–11 is the classic New Testament passage on that theme. Read those words from the apostle Paul.

a. Where do you see the elements of both a powerful king and a suffering servant?

b. What does it mean to have the same attitude as Christ (v. 5)?

c. How are you doing at living out verses 3 and 4?

d. Are you experiencing a situation in which you sense that God is asking you to be a "suffering servant"?

 DAYLIGHT ON PRAYER

Spending Time with God

1. How can the group pray for you to be more like Christ, the suffering servant?

2. What other prayer requests do you have for the group?

3. Open your Bible to Isaiah 52:13–53:12. Offer up to God prayers of thanks and praise based on portions of this incredible Scripture passage.

 ## DAYLIGHT AHEAD

Why does it seem that those people who loved Jesus so much—who just days before had hailed Him as King at the triumphal entry—choose to crucify Him? As Avner Boskey and Meno Kalisher see it, it was not those people who caused Jesus to be sent to the cross. It was the higher officials who acted as the people slept. But in reality, it was not a group of people who are to be blamed. It was a victory of God that His plan was carried out at the cross. Messiah, the Anointed One. Jesus, the Savior of the world. That's who He was and is.

Who Is This Messiah?

DAYLIGHT PREVIEW

Jesus: A Popular Figure

From the crowds lining the streets of Jerusalem, "Hosanna!" rang out as Jesus slowly rode through the city. This Man, who had commanded large crowds wherever He went because of His message and His healings, was being heralded as a coming King. Indeed Jesus was popular with the people. But behind the crowd stood the officials, the religious leaders who did not look too kindly at this visitor from Nazareth. Through fear or misunderstanding they sought to thwart this Messiah and stop Him from being loved and worshiped by the people. Little did those leaders know that they were playing right into God's hands, for it was through Jesus' death that victory would come.

—————————— COME TOGETHER ——————————

Icebreaker Questions

1. Jesus was a very popular figure. Who do you remember as "Mr. Popular" or "Miss Popular" in your high school?

2. Avner notes that Jesus' appearance before Pilate occurred about five o'clock the morning after the Passover meal, when most people would be asleep. How well do you usually sleep the night after Christmas? How

well do you usually sleep the night *before* Christmas? How about when you were a child?

3. Avner also notes that some Jews view the Messiah kind of like a Jewish "Santa Claus," somebody who will give gifts and make everything right, but who knows if he'll really show up on Christmas morning? What did you believe about Santa Claus when you were a child?

FINDING DAYLIGHT

Experience the Video

Feel free to jot down Video Notes as you watch the presentation by Mart De Haan, Meno Kalisher, and Avner Boskey. Use the space below for those notes.

─────────────────────VIDEO NOTES─────────────────────

The popularity of Jesus

The rejection of Jesus

The back story

Power politics in Jesus' day

God's strategy in Isaiah 53

Who killed Jesus?

Modern Jewish thinking about Messiah

What should we be thinking for today?

Salvation

Restoration

Meno and Messiah

God's order

Mart's summary

Does it matter?

WALKING IN THE DAYLIGHT

Discussion Time

——————————— DISCOVER GOD'S WORD ———————————

Discussion/Application Questions

1. This session begins with a reference to the triumphal entry on what
    we call Palm Sunday. Read Matthew's account of that story in Mat-
    thew 21:1–11.

    Why do you think Jesus was popular with the common people but
    rejected by the religious leaders?

2. The attitude of the crowd on Palm Sunday was much different from
    the attitude of the crowd when Jesus was brought before Pilate on
    Good Friday. Read Mark's account of that scene in Mark 15:1–15.

a. What do you think of Avner's analysis that the people who cried "Hosanna" on the Mount of Olives on Palm Sunday virtually weren't involved in Jesus' arrest, trial, and crucifixion—but later took the attitude, "Well, we're going to follow our leaders"?

b. This led Mart, Avner, and Meno to a discussion of who killed Jesus. What do you think of Meno's position that rather than focusing on the question of blame we should focus on the reality that Jesus came to die on the cross and that Jesus' death on the cross is the plan and victory of God?

3. **According to Avner, about 70 to 80 percent of all Jews are secular and don't believe a Messiah is coming.**

    Does that surprise you? Why?

4. **Avner goes on to say that those who do believe a Messiah is coming (Orthodox Jews and some Conservative Jews) expect that the Messiah will restore Israel from exile, defeat all of Israel's enemies, and rebuild the temple.**

    Why do you think their expectation doesn't include a focus on a Messiah who is going to redeem His people from their sins?

5. Mart asks Meno and Avner, "From your understanding of the Bible, both Old and New Testament, where do you think our minds *should be* when it comes to a right understanding of Messiah for today and for the future?" Both answered that the primary emphasis should be that Jesus came in order to pay for the sins not only of Jews but also of the whole world, so that anyone can get into right relationship with God through Jesus.

    How do you feel about Avner's view that a restoration of God's government on earth is also coming through the return of the King, the son of David?

6. As this session and series nears its conclusion, Mart notes that when the time came for Jesus to reveal His identity and to explain the meaning of His life and death, He pointed His followers to His roots in the Jewish Scriptures. Read Luke 24:13–24, the first part of the story involving two followers of Jesus who were walking from Jerusalem to Emmaus on Easter Sunday.

    One of these two disciples was Cleopas (v. 18), not one of the inner circle of twelve disciples. The other person wasn't named, but in light of verse 33 evidently was also not included in the "Eleven" (i.e., the "Twelve" now minus Judas Iscariot). By divine intervention, they were kept from recognizing Jesus (v. 16).

    a. Why do you suppose these two followers of Jesus seemed reluctant to call Him the Messiah?

b. What was their expectation regarding Jesus' mission?

7. Read how this story ended in Luke 24:25–32.

a. What did Jesus want these two disciples to know from the Jewish Scriptures?

b. What effect did His explanation of the Scriptures have on them?

8. Read what happened next as these two disciples returned to Jerusalem in Luke 24:33–49.

a. How did Jesus calm His friends' fears and prove that it was really Him who was in their presence?

b. Again, what did Jesus want His disciples to know from the Jewish Scriptures?

Meno shares that talking about the Messiah is not just a Jewish or religious issue. "For me, Messiah means a personal relationship with God: a relationship that is taking care of my sin, giving me freedom to serve Him, giving me the possibility of calling Him Father—*Abba*. I can knock on the door, God opens it, and I run to Him, saying, 'Hello, Father!'"

How do you feel about the quality of your relationship with God? Has it been getting more intimate or less intimate?

DAYLIGHT ON PRAYER

Spending Time with God

1. What have you appreciated the most about this series and this group?

2. How can the group continue to support you in prayer?

3. As you conclude your prayer time, thank God for His wonderful plan of giving the world a Messiah and that through that Messiah, the Lord Jesus Christ, we can know God intimately as our heavenly Father.